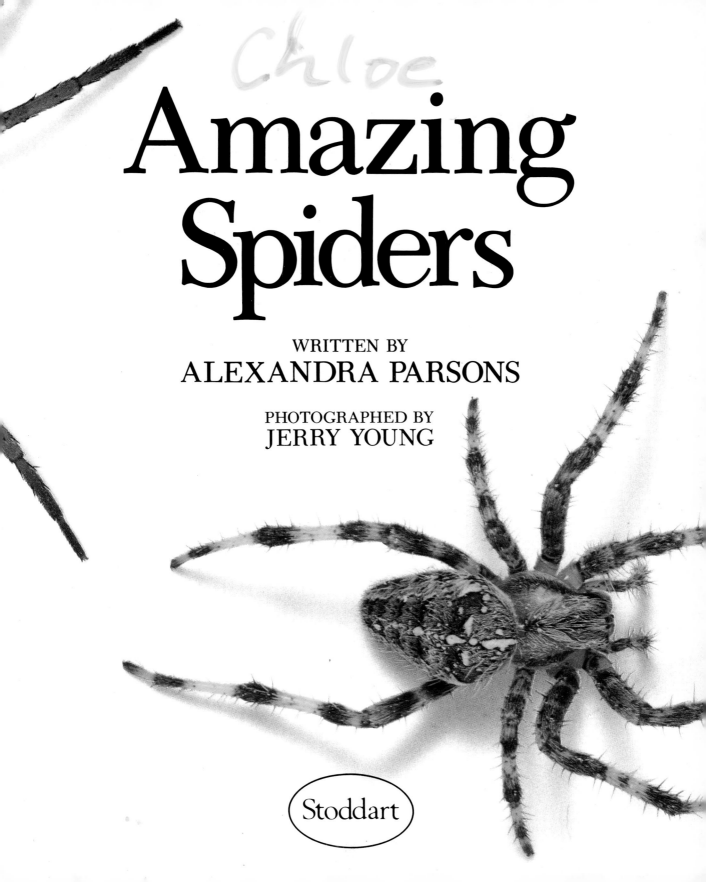

Chloe

Amazing
Spiders

WRITTEN BY
ALEXANDRA PARSONS

PHOTOGRAPHED BY
JERRY YOUNG

Stoddart

Editor Scott Steedman
Designers Ann Cannings and Margo Beamish-White
Senior art editor Jacquie Gulliver
Editorial director Sue Unstead
Art director Anne-Marie Bulat

Special photography by Jerry Young
Illustrations by Mark Iley, John Davis, and Polly Noakes
Animals supplied by Trevor Smith's Animal World
Editorial consultants
The staff of the Natural History Museum, London

Published in Great Britain by Dorling Kindersley Limited
9 Henrietta Street, London, England WC2E 8PS

First published in Canada in 1990 by Stoddart Publishing Co. Limited
34 Lesmill Road, Toronto, Canada M3B 2T6

Canadian Cataloguing in Publication Data
Parsons, Alexandra
Amazing spiders

(Amazing worlds series)
ISBN 0-7737-2394-3

1. Spiders - Juvenile literature. I. Title.
II. Series: Parsons, Alexandra. Amazing
worlds series.

QL452.2.P37 1990   j595.4'4   C89-090/89-7

Color reproduction by Colourscan, Singapore
Typeset by Windsorgraphics, Ringwood, Hampshire
Printed in Italy by A. Mondadori Editore, Verona

Contents

What is a spider?

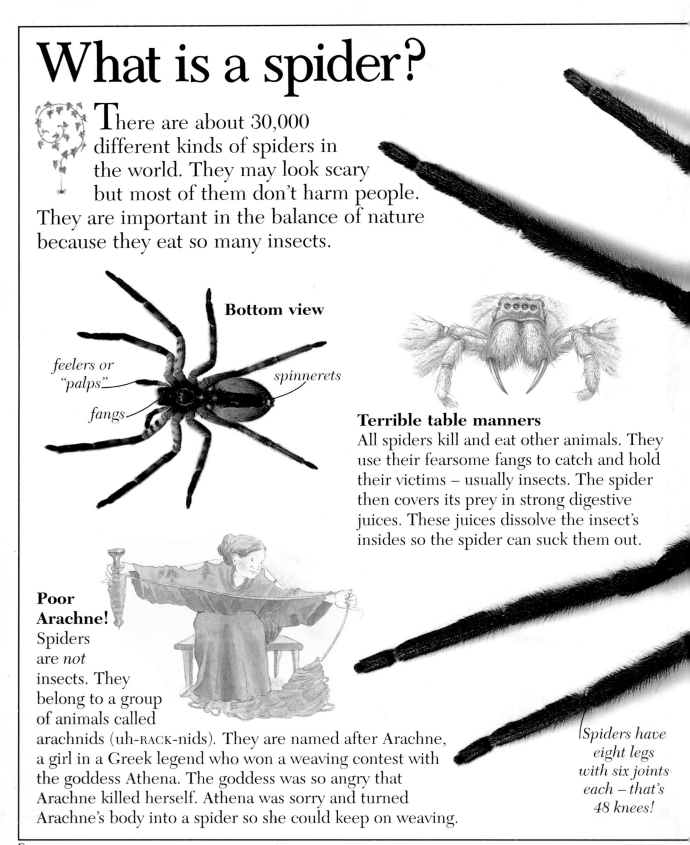

There are about 30,000 different kinds of spiders in the world. They may look scary but most of them don't harm people. They are important in the balance of nature because they eat so many insects.

Bottom view

feelers or "palps"

spinnerets

fangs

Terrible table manners

All spiders kill and eat other animals. They use their fearsome fangs to catch and hold their victims – usually insects. The spider then covers its prey in strong digestive juices. These juices dissolve the insect's insides so the spider can suck them out.

Poor Arachne!

Spiders are *not* insects. They belong to a group of animals called arachnids (uh-RACK-nids). They are named after Arachne, a girl in a Greek legend who won a weaving contest with the goddess Athena. The goddess was so angry that Arachne killed herself. Athena was sorry and turned Arachne's body into a spider so she could keep on weaving.

Spiders have eight legs with six joints each – that's 48 knees!

A spider does not have bones. Its tough skin, or cuticle, acts as a protective outer skeleton.

Eye spy
Most spiders have two rows of four eyes each, or eight eyes altogether.

fine silk thread from spinneret

spinnerets

Spider webbing
Spiders spin their silk with tiny organs called spinnerets. The silk starts as a sticky liquid which hardens in the air to form a thread that is light but strong.

The two main parts of a spider's body are the joined head and chest at the front and the abdomen at the back.

Nonslip feet
Many spiders can walk up walls and across ceilings because they have special grip-pads on their feet.

Spare skin
As a spider grows, its hard outer skin becomes too tight. It sheds the whole skin, first cracking it open on the back and then climbing out of it.

9

Friends of the earth

The most common spiders on earth are the house spider and the garden spider. If you see them, don't kill them. They help keep your house and garden free of bugs.

Sticky center
The garden spider spins a beautiful spiral web designed to catch flying insects. The center is made of a special sticky silk so insects that fly into it can't fly out.

The large palps are very sensitive to vibrations in the spider's web.

Munch, munch!
There are billions and billions of spiders in the world. If every spider ate just one insect a day for a year and you piled up all those insects in one spot, they would weigh as much as 50 million people!

Two of this garden spider's eyes are on top of its head.

Perfect pet
The house spider makes a good pet. You won't have to feed it too often – a fly a day is more than enough. A spider needs water, so give it a damp sponge to suck.

Close to mother
Some female spiders lay their eggs in a silk cocoon. The spider carries this with her, scurrying around her web with the ball of silk hanging from her abdomen.

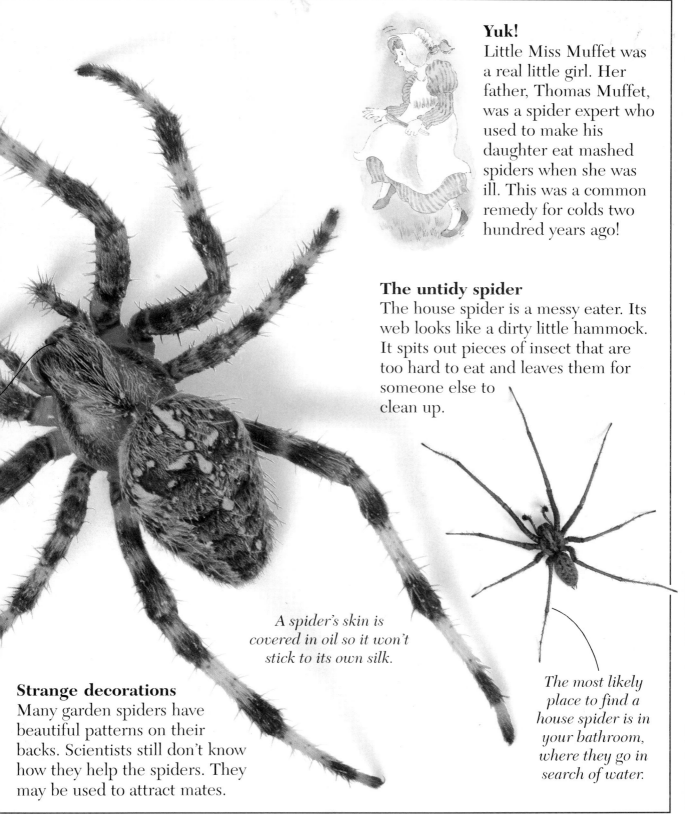

Yuk!

Little Miss Muffet was a real little girl. Her father, Thomas Muffet, was a spider expert who used to make his daughter eat mashed spiders when she was ill. This was a common remedy for colds two hundred years ago!

The untidy spider

The house spider is a messy eater. Its web looks like a dirty little hammock. It spits out pieces of insect that are too hard to eat and leaves them for someone else to clean up.

A spider's skin is covered in oil so it won't stick to its own silk.

The most likely place to find a house spider is in your bathroom, where they go in search of water.

Strange decorations

Many garden spiders have beautiful patterns on their backs. Scientists still don't know how they help the spiders. They may be used to attract mates.

Giant, hairy spiders

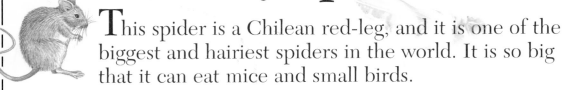

This spider is a Chilean red-leg, and it is one of the biggest and hairiest spiders in the world. It is so big that it can eat mice and small birds.

Seeing and feeling
Spiders may have a lot of eyes, but most can't see very well. Very sensitive hairs on their legs and feelers help them find their way.

Dance the tarantella
Not all large, hairy spiders are tarantulas. The real tarantula is a big, poisonous spider from Italy. People used to believe that dancing was the only cure for the spider's bite. The dance became known as the tarantella.

Hairy scary
When it is attacked, the red-leg will tear the prickly hairs off its back and fling them at its attacker.

Eek!
Being terrified of spiders is called arachnophobia (uh-RACK-no-FOE-bee-uh).

Strong legs used to dig burrows

Little and large
The world's smallest spider lives on the Pacific island of Samoa. It is so small that it would fit on the period at the end of this sentence. The biggest spider of all lurks in the jungles of South America. With its legs stretched out it measures 10 inches – about the size of a dinner plate.

Old-age pensioners
Female tarantulas have been known to live for over 25 years. Most males die by the age of nine or 10.

Facts about fangs
Most spiders have fangs that swing together, grasping their prey like a pair of pliers. Big spiders such as tarantulas have downward-pointing fangs for pinning down their lunch.

Most male spiders have smaller bodies than females, but their legs are just as long.

Water spiders

Spiders that live in or on the water still need to breathe air. One water spider traps bubbles of air in an underwater web, where it lives and lays its eggs.

The diving bell

The water spider spins a web in the shape of a bell underneath the water. It fills the bell with a bubble of air and anchors it to a piece of water weed. This air pocket is the spider's underwater home.

You can tell a raft spider by the pale bands on the sides of its dark body.

Refilling the tanks

When its underwater web needs more air, the hardworking water spider goes up to the surface and traps tiny bubbles in the hairs of its body. Then it zips back home and lets go of the air bubbles inside its tiny web.

Like most spiders, the raft spider has tiny claws at the end of its feet.

The crafty raft spider

This spider lives by the water's edge. Although it is big, it can walk on water without sinking. It does this by spreading its legs wide and taking quick, gentle steps.

A new wardrobe

Like all spiders, the raft spider sheds its skin as it gets bigger. When the growing spider crawls out of its old skin, or cuticle, it is covered in a layer of new skin. It sits in the sun for a few hours while the new skin hardens.

New legs

If a spider loses a leg (and they often do), it can simply grow a new one.

Gone fishing

The swamp spider lives on the surface of the water, where it catches and eats tiny minnows. To attract its prey, the spider dabbles its feet in the water. When the unsuspecting fish rise to the surface, the spider pounces and in go the fangs.

Jack-in-the-box

Trapdoor spiders and purse web spiders live in burrows. Each spider builds a silken trap around the mouth of its den. When a tasty meal strolls by, the spider leaps out like a jack-in-the-box.

Lair with a lid
A trapdoor spider spends most of its time in its underground burrow, waiting for a bug to pass its door.

The spare room
Some trapdoor spiders dig several "rooms" in their burrows. One will be a dining room, one may be a nursery, and one will be a safe place to stay during a flood.

This spider has shiny armor plating on its head and chest to protect its insides. The velvety abdomen is much softer.

Neighbors
Burrowing spiders such as the trapdoor spider live alone, one to a burrow. Several spiders may live close together but they don't do it to be neighborly – they do it because the area is good for building burrows.

Bugs in the pantry

If spiders catch an insect when they're not hungry, they will poison it without killing it and wrap it up in silk. Then they can be sure of a nice fresh meal whenever they feel hungry again.

Built-in plug

One kind of trapdoor spider has a body shaped like the nose cone of a rocket. When it is chased, it bolts down its hole and plugs up the entrance with its hard, flat behind.

Trapdoor spiders are found mainly in warm, tropical regions – this one is from the southern United States.

A silken prison

The female purse web spider lives in a silken pouch that spills out of her burrow. When an insect stumbles on her trap, she slices the pouch open and sinks in her fangs.

Jumpers and spitters

Not all spiders catch their meals in webs. Some jump on their prey, and others spit out a sticky net of poison.

What muscles!
A jumping spider can leap 40 times its body length.

The legs of a jumping spider are short and very, very strong.

Safety rope
The jumping spider (above) hunts insects like a cat hunts mice. But before it jumps on its prey, the spider anchors itself to the ground with a silk thread.

Slow but sure
The spitting spider (left) moves very slowly, but it can catch even a speedy fly. The spider spits out a net of poison and glue that takes the insect completely by surprise and pins it to the ground.

Deadly shy

The black widow is a shy little spider that doesn't like to fight. That's why it has such deadly poison. If a scorpion or a lizard gets stuck in its web, all the spider has to do is nip the scorpion's leg, stand back, and wham! Lunch is ready.

Bringing up baby

The black widow glues her egg sac to a branch and waits for the eggs to hatch. The baby spiders will have nothing to eat but each other until they are big enough to build webs of their own. Out of 100 baby spiders, maybe 25 will survive.

Funnel of death

The Australian funnel web spider is one of the world's deadliest. It is big and black, with hairy legs and huge fangs so strong they can pierce bone.

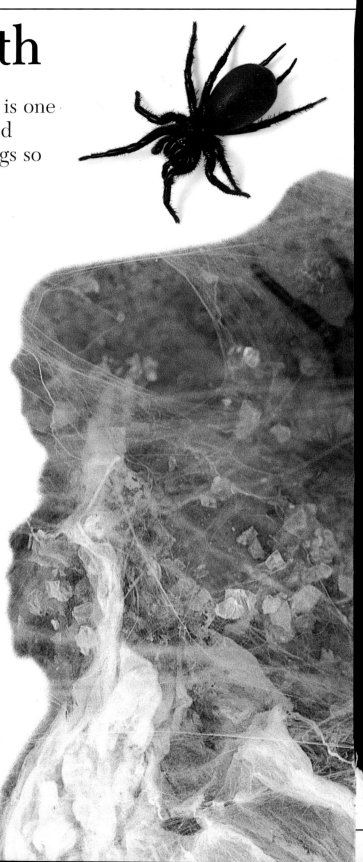

Poison fangs
All spiders have poisonous bites, but some are more poisonous than others. Luckily scientists have now made special medicines that can cure people who have been badly bitten.

Hard to kill
Sprays that would kill other spiders just make funnel webs angry.

Silky sheets
The funnel web lives underground where it is cool and damp. It lines its burrow with sheets of silk and sleeps through the winter.

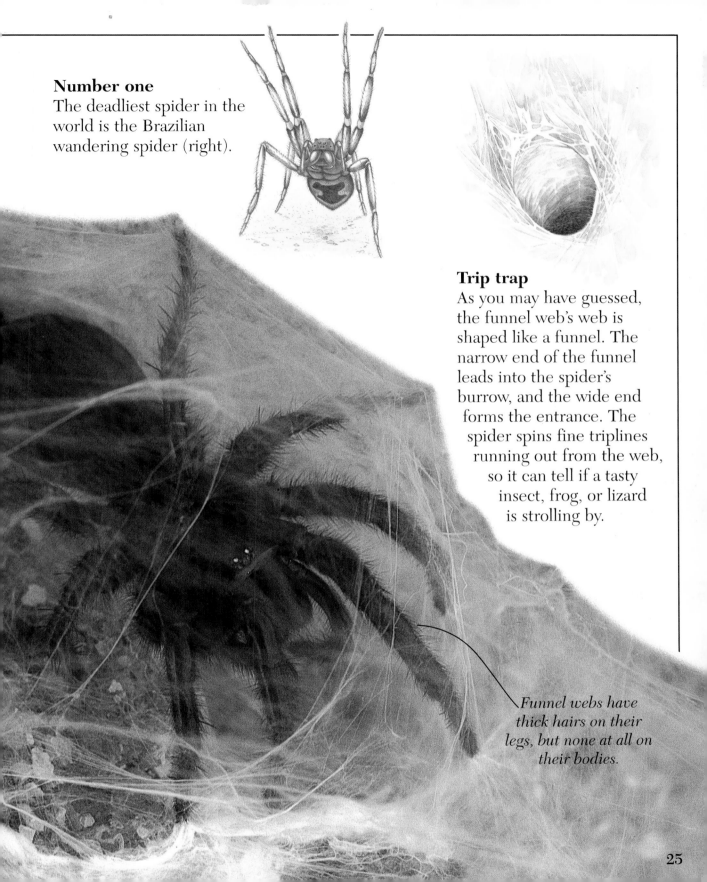

Number one
The deadliest spider in the world is the Brazilian wandering spider (right).

Trip trap
As you may have guessed, the funnel web's web is shaped like a funnel. The narrow end of the funnel leads into the spider's burrow, and the wide end forms the entrance. The spider spins fine triplines running out from the web, so it can tell if a tasty insect, frog, or lizard is strolling by.

Funnel webs have thick hairs on their legs, but none at all on their bodies.

The weavers

Orb weaver spiders spin beautiful, intricate webs. The webs are shaped like targets and are strung between two supports.

Can spiders fly?
Spiders don't have wings, so they cannot actually fly. But some tiny spiders are blown about by the wind. Using silk threads like little parachutes, they can travel on the breeze for hundreds of miles.

Speedy spider
The fastest spider in the world can run 330 times its own body length in 10 seconds. A person can only manage 50 times his body length in that time.

Silk or steel?
If you made a steel thread as fine as a thread of spider silk, the silk would be three times stronger.

Young spinners
Each kind of spider builds its own kind of web. The moment a spider hatches from its egg, it knows how to spin a certain pattern, just as you were born knowing how to cry and how to suck.

To spin its web, the black orb weaver spider uses a thread of silk so long it would wrap around this book 50 times.

First aid
Some people put a clean spider's web on a cut or wound to stop the bleeding and help the cut to heal.

The bristles on a spider's legs help it feel vibrations in the air – or on its web.

Fishing nets
There is a spider called *Nephila* that lives in very hot countries. The webs it makes are so thick and so strong that the local people collect the webs and use them as fishing nets.

How to spin a web

It takes a spider about an hour to spin an orb web like this. The fine silk thread looks delicate, but it can hold 4,000 times the spider's own weight!

1 First the spider spins a thread between two supports – helped, perhaps, by a breeze that blows the thread across. Then it spins another and dangles from the middle.

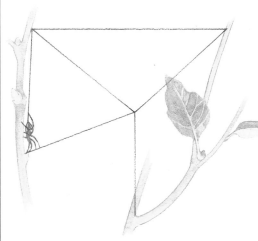

2 Next it drops a new thread to make a Y-shape, and spins more threads from the center to the edge.

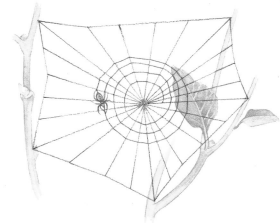

3 Then the spider spins around and around in a spiral, working slowly out from the middle.

4 Finally it spirals back into the center and sits and waits there for an insect to fly by.

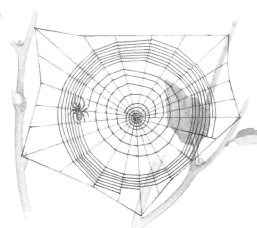

Spiders have to repair their fragile webs all the time because careless insects keep flying into them!

Trip wire

Spiders often lie in wait with one leg on a "signal thread." When an unsuspecting victim lands in the web, the thread shakes. Instantly, the spider pounces.

Index